D1514822

LITTLE BO-PEEP HAS
KNICKERS THAT BLEEP

Laurence Anholt wrote the rhymes,
Arthur Robins drew the lines.

ORCHARD BOOKS

If you're very bored indeed,
Here's some stuff for you to read:

This magnificent little book was
published by those CHARMING people at

ORCHARD BOOKS

who all live together at:
96 Leonard Street, London EC2A 4XD
(You can send them a Christmas card if you like.)

Published down under by
Orchard Books Australia
32/45-51 Huntley Street, Alexandria, NSW 2015

First published in Great Britain in 2002. First paperback edition 2003

Blah, blah, blahdy blah...

Don't steal the words, man.

Arthur's drawings: HANDS OFF!

Dooby dooby dooby doo··

A CIP catalogue record for this book is available from the British Library.

etc, etc...

Does anyone read this stuff?

ISBN 1 84121 016 1 (hardback)
ISBN 1 84121 024 2 (paperback)
1 3 5 7 9 10 8 6 4 2 (hardback)
1 3 5 7 9 10 8 6 4 2 (paperback)

ARE YOU STILL THERE?

Printed in Great Britain

Goodnight.

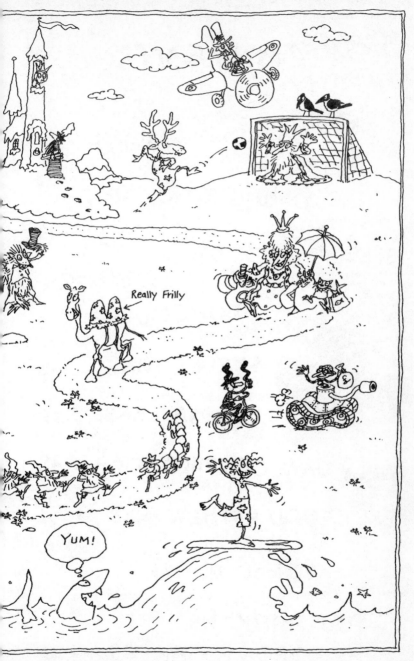

Really Frilly

YUM!

the Man ☆ Johnny Stout ☆ Little Bo-Peep ☆ The Queen
ry, Mary ☆ The Deadly Dinner Ladies ☆ Greedy Green Martian

CONTENTS

GOB-SMACKING GOBLINS

Ten green goblins
Reading on a wall.
Ten green goblins,
Smiley, fat and small.

And if nine green goblins
Should slip in sloppy slime...

There'd be one green goblin
With his *Seriously Silly Rhymes.*

BOOMING BLOOMERS

Little Bo Peep has knickers that bleep,
So that her lambies can find her.
"Beep beep," says Bo Peep, "Baa baa,"
    say the sheep,
Skipping along behind her.

Wherever Bo goes, her underwear
    glows,
So that her lambies won't lose her.
These knickers are neat, they heat up
    her seat
And play groovy tunes to amuse her.

Little Bo Peepy, was feeling quite
   sleepy,
A cup of hot cocoa inside her.
"I'll turn up that dial," she said with
   a smile,
And the lambies curled up beside her.

But...

At eleven o'clock, the flock got a shock
As the powerful panties corroded.
A woolly white sheep had weed in its
    sleep,
And those magical knickers exploded.

STREET-WISE PETE

Diddle, diddle, dumpling, my son Pete,
Pushed his bed out in the street.
The road was busy, the hill was steep,
My son Pete was *fast* asleep.

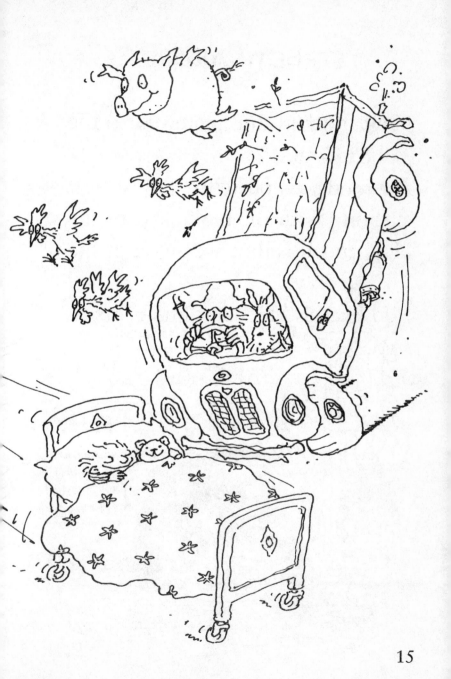

HOWL MUCH?

How much is that werewolf in the
    window?
Ho-oo-wl, ho-oo-wl!
The one with the really sharp claws.
How much is that werewolf in the
    window?
I do like his bloodcurdling roars.

How much is that werewolf in the
    window?
Haroo-oo-oo-oow!
The one with the chin full of drool.
How much is that werewolf in the
    window?
I would like that wolfie at school.

SKELLY TUNE

A skinny young fellow named Tony
Said, "My diet's a load of baloney.
    Whatever I eat,
    Ends up by my feet.
If only I wasn't so bony."

LOADSA LEGS

Oh where, oh where, has my
    millipede gone?
His ears are quite short but his legs go
on and on and on and on and on and
on and on and on and on...

*A footnote: This poem is over 100 feet long.

SILLY DAYS OF CHRISTMAS

On the first day of Christmas,
My girlfriend sent to me:
A parsnip in a pot of tea.

On the second day of Christmas,
I sent my girlfriend back:
Two tins of toes
And a parcel for a bumblebee.

On the third day of Christmas,
My girlfriend sent to me:
Three twirling thieves,
Two tiger twins
And a party for a chimpanzee.

I'll put them under
the Christmas tree.

On the fourth day of Christmas,
I sent my girlfriend back:
Four fat fairies,

Three throbbing thumbs,

Two trucks of toilets,

And a parachute for a purple flea.

On the fifth day of Christmas,
My girlfriend sent to me:

Five co-o-old kings,

Four fish fingers,
Three thin thongs,
Two tipsy turtles,
And a parasol for a referee.

23

On the sixth day of Christmas,
I sent my girlfriend back:
Six sandals singing,

Five mi-i-les of string,

Four fake feet,
Three thrushes thinking,
Two talking trout,
And a parka for a Cherokee.

On the seventh day of Christmas,
My girlfriend sent to me:
Seven socks a-swimming,
Six square squirrels,
Five o-o-old bins,
Four fields of flowers,
Three thatched theatres,
Two tiny trolls,
And a plaster for my mother's knee.

Let's save them for next year.

On the eighth day of Christmas,
I sent my girlfriend back:
Eight amazing mazes,
Seven snakes a-smiling,
Six Shakespeare's shaving,
Five bo-o-ld chins,
Four French families,
Three thumping thugs,
Two tadpole teeth,
And a fastener from her dungarees.

On the ninth day of Christmas,
My true love sent to me:
Ninety nuns a-nunning,
Eighty apes a-peeling,
Seventy sacks of salad,
Sixty *Seriously Silly Stories*,
Fifty mo-o-uldy things,
Forty farting frogs,
Thirty thousand thermometers,
Twenty tons of trash,
And a parson on a plastic ski.

FAST FOOD FATHER

Bye, baby bunting,
Daddy's gone a-hunting.

Daddy's not so brave today,
He's come back with a take-away.

Mum doesn't call us for dinner –
we just wait for the smoke alarm.

POT SHOT

A goalie who played for West Ham
Was so young that he came with his
    mam.
    He let in a shot,
    As he sat on his pot,
But the ball ended up in his pram.

D'YOU THINK THE BRONTO SAW US?

When you are safely sleeping,
You might not hear their roars.
The garden's full of monsters
And great green carnivores.
Dinosaurs eat dustbins
And they don't take off the lids.
The Brontosaurus bites up beds
And this one's full of kids.

A WEIRD WEEK OR WHAT?

Monday's child is nice to eat,

Tuesday's child has fifteen feet,

Wednesday's child is big and blue,

Thursday's child is a kangaroo,

Friday's child is wild and weird,

Saturday's child has a purple beard,

And the child that is born on the
     Sabbath day
Has a nose as long as a motorway.

BOGEY BOY

Little Jack Horner
Sat in a corner,
Picking his little pink nose.
He said,

Incey Wincey spider dialled up the
    internet.
Down came his dad in a major sweat.
Up came his mum and tried hard to
    explain.
Then Incey Wincey spider went on
    the web again.

THE BATTY BATTERY RAP

WARNING!
Do not try this at home.*
*Any damage is your own volt.

Oh dear, what can the matter be?
My dad swallowed a battery,

He's normally rather less chattery,
Look at the lights in his hair.

CANDLE VANDAL

Jack was nimble,
Jack was quick,
Jack jumped over the candlestick.
Silly lad, he should've jumped higher,
Jack has set his pants on fire.

Jack was nimble,
But rather slow,
Jack jumped over a volcano.

Goodness gracious! What a palaver!
Jack has sat in red hot lava.

Jack was nimble,
Jack was cool,
Jack dived into a swimming pool.
Silly little Jack,
You know you oughta...
Check the pool is
Full of water.

BARE ON THE STAIR

Row, row, row your bottom,
Gently down the stairs.
Merrily, merrily, merrily, merrily,
In your underwear.

A SAD TAIL

There was a little girl and she had a
   little curl
Right in the middle of her bottom.

> I once had a line
>   To end this rhyme,
> But I'm afraid
>   That I've forgotten.

A REALLY RUDE RHYME

A moody old dude from Bude
Said, "I find people terribly rude.
    It's true that I'm bare
    But there's no need to stare."
And he chewed his food in the nude.

COOL CLOUD CAROL

Hark! The herald angel sings,

We are cool, 'cos we got wings.

Buzzing round the sky so blue,
Wings are kind of stylish too.
So come on all you angel guys,
Join the party in the skies.
If the music gets too loud,
Block your ears with bits of cloud.

Hark! The choirs and heavenly chimes,

ALL ABOUT
THE AUTHOR

LAURENCE

Laurence Anholt looks like this:
He loves to eat spaghetti.
He takes a nap at half-past three,
And dreams he is a yeti.

His nose is long, his legs are thin,
He lives beside the sea.
He never dances in the nude
When he has friends for tea.

He burns the dinner when he cooks,
He likes to wear disguise.
He writes those *Seriously Silly* books
Which won the Smarties Prize.*

*LAURENCE
IN
DISGUISE*

* Smarties Gold Award

ALL ABOUT
THE ILLUSTRATOR

Arthur Robins keeps his paint
In tiny, dinky pots.
He has a really nice white suit
That's splashed with inky spots.

He chats to Laurence on the phone,
They share a simple joke.
He works inside a garden shed
Not far from Basingstoke.

Arthur's really famous now,
On that we all agree.
So if you meet him in the street
Please go down on one knee.

SERIOUSLY SILLY RHYMES and STORIES

Laurence Anholt ☆ Arthur Robins

All priced at £3.99

Seriously Silly books are available from all good bookshops,
or can be ordered direct from the publisher:
Orchard Books, PO BOX 29, Douglas IM99 1BQ
Credit card orders please telephone 01624 836000
or fax 01624 837033
or e-mail: bookshop@enterprise.net for details.

To order please quote title, author and ISBN
and your full name and address.
Cheques and postal orders should be
made payable to 'Bookpost plc'.

Postage and packing is FREE within the UK
(overseas customers should add £1.00 per book).

Prices and availability are subject to change.